CW01670164

JUKEBOXES

The Golden Age

JUKEBOXES

The Golden Age

Text by Vincent Lynch and Bill Henkin

Photographs by Kazuhiro Tsuruta

Preface by David Rubinson

Thames and Hudson

We would like to especially acknowledge the following people without whose diligent work this book would have been impossible to present.

John Garlow

Jim Liljenwal

Tom Barrett

Avi Weisbach

John Sala

Andy Lasky

John Mayer

And, for their assistance in the research and preparation of the book we thank:

Eddie Adlum
Russell Allard
Anna Bjorn
Busse
Tom Cantella
Michael Del Castello
Howard Dolph
Dan Driskell
Bob Fulwider
Eldon Garrett
Larry Johnson
Judith
Koichiro Kawahara
Steve Loots
Clyde Love
Jakeb Magnussen
Russ Ofria
Ken Oilschlager
A.D. Palmer, Jr.
Dave Palmer
Dawn Patrick
Howard Pearlstein
Brad Pueschel
Richard Rodriquez
Murray Salerno
Joel Selvin
Kay Steinhauer
Johnny Vincent
Maurice White
Bill Worthy

Contents

Preface

My relationship with the jukebox has gone the way of many affairs. At first I cast coy glances out of the corner of my eye at the object of my affection and I finally worked up the nerve to stare full-faced at the beauty against the wall. It was love. My feelings grew and soon one jukebox, or two, or ten, wasn't enough. I loved the *Peacock* for its showy grace, the *1015* for its accessibility and bubbly good humor, dependable but fun. I could not resist the sloping shoulders of the *950* or even the ugly, squat pugnaciousness of the *Seeburg Barrel*.

I've seen grown men cry over a *Singing Towers* and innocent children stare transfixed for hours into the face of a *Rock-Ola 1426*. I've watched a team of gifted surgeons, impassioned beyond skill, labor feverishly over a mangled heap of wood, glass, tubes, wires and metal, to turn a pile of junk into a gleaming, working machine. This is how most of my beauties are born. Best of all, they sing! They sing mostly of another time—of Dry Bones, Moonlight Serenade and Heartbreak Hotel; of Tutti-Frutti and Stormy Monday; One O'Clock Jump and Sixty Minute Man; of Strange Fruit, Little Susie and Annie Had a Baby.

My love affair with the jukebox may have its roots in the space-age environment in which I work every day, in computerized recording studios surrounded by million-dollar machines. The sound is fabulous, but nothing beats hearing an old 78 on the machine on which it was born to be played. The music I make every day finds its true expression on supersonic state-of-the-art gear, or on the radio. Duke Ellington sounds best to me on my *Wurlitzer*.

The biggest surprise of my affair was finding out how many other people share my obsession. Thousands of crazed lovers all over the world tinker endlessly, haggle over a pane of *Victory* glass or a bubble tube, craft their own parts where none still exist, buy and sell, trade and retrade—a fanatical sub-culture in stark contrast to the mass-merchandising commerce of modern life. When I realized how many of us there were I felt a twinge of jealousy. But the jukebox lover is not a jealous lover. We collectors compete in our ardor, but we share our love. For the people who already share this deep affection and for those who through these pages may fall as I did years ago, this book is a testimony to that love.

David Rubinson

JUKEBOXES

The Golden Age

In 1877, while trying to invent the telegraph machine, Thomas Alva Edison incidentally discovered sound recording. The machine Edison developed was completely mechanical. It recorded by impressing sound wave modulations onto a sheet of tinfoil, used no electricity in either its recording or its playback functions, and—in the absence of electrical amplification—had no speakers. Sound was reproduced acoustically, and heard through a listening tube.

Edison, before going on to invent the light bulb, sold the rights to manufacture his tinfoil phonograph for $10,000 plus a 20% royalty. He maintained a distant interest in the Edison Speaking Phonograph, urging that it be used as a business machine—a primitive sort of Dictaphone—while only tolerating its exploitation as an entertainment medium.

But Edison miscalculated the desires of the American public; and it was, in fact, an Edison machine that was fitted out with a coin slot by Louis Glass, and installed at the Palais Royale Saloon in San Francisco, California on November 23, 1889, as the official first coin-operated phonograph.

The phonograph Glass installed had four listening tubes; each was to be put to the ear of a single listener, and each required a nickel to make music for perhaps two minutes. This precursor to the jukebox could never have had the cultural impact its descendents came to have, simply because it could only be heard by a few people at a time. Nonetheless, as an amusement its novelty so piqued the curiosity of the public that it quickly became the basis for a thriving industry. Three months after Glass's installation the Automatic Phonograph Exhibition Company of New York was making coin-operated music machine components; later in 1890 the Columbia Phonograph Company turned its attention to the problems of making cylinder recordings—the first commercial records; and by 1891 the Louisiana Phonograph Company claimed that a single one of its machines, which cost about two hundred dollars, had grossed more than one thousand dollars in a two-month period.

The recording stars of this first phonograph era were John Philip Sousa's Marine Band, and John Y. At Lee, who whistled three dozen tunes onto Columbia's lists in a single year. Along with the recordings of numerous balladeers and comedians, Sousa's stirring marches and At Lee's airy flourishes were heard in the phonograph parlors that sprang up from New York to Paris in the late 1890s, extending the range and impact of the recording novelty. In Pathe's salon in Paris, for example, the customer sat at one of about forty desks, each of which was equipped with its own listening tube. After depositing a coin into the slot, the patron spoke into the tube and requested any of fifteen hundred selections. On the floor below, the original disk jockeys played each customer's song on a phonograph wired to that particular phonograph's ear tube.

After several years the popular novelty of the phonograph parlor wore off. By the first years of the new century they were becoming the province of gumball machines, slot sports, and grifters. Known then as "penny arcades," they ceased attracting the better classes of clientelle, and fell into disrepute. Briefly, the player piano replaced the phonograph parlor as the central attraction in the mechanized music world, and nearly strangled the fledgling phonograph industry.

In 1906 the John Gabel Company brought out the most important new coin-operated music machine to that time. The Gabel Automatic Entertainer was the first coin-operated music machine to offer more than one selection, and among the first to use ten-inch disks instead of wax-and-cardboard cylinders; its record-changing mechanism could be viewed through the three glass sides at the top of its oak cabinet; its sophisticated coin slot mechanism could distinguish slugs from real money; a forty-inch horn amplified its sound enough so that anyone nearby could hear its music without the aid of a listening tube; and, although it still had to be hand-wound, all its subsequent operations were fully automatic. In all, the Entertainer was so richly innovative it is generally considered to be the true forerunner of the modern jukebox. This machine, and variations of it, dominated the coin-op phonograph industry for the next twenty years.

Technology did not catch up with the jukebox until 1927, when several companies introduced electrically amplified instruments, and the Automatic Music Instrument Company (AMI) released the industry's first electrically amplified multi-selection phonograph. Electrical amplification was the single most important technical improvement in the history of the machine. It created something entirely different from what had come before, and made possible everything that followed. Suddenly the jukebox was capable of competing with loud orchestras. It could entertain large groups of people in large halls, all at once, for a nickel.

This innovation did not take place in a vacuum. Between 1906 and 1927 radio had become a major industry. In 1919 the Victor Talking Machine Company claimed $26 million from the sale of crystal receiver sets alone. And the force of radio's success opened the door for the electrically amplified coin phonograph.

By the late 20s people were becoming increasingly mobile in the nation. They sought an expressive music to reflect their new dimensions. Just before the outbreak of the first world war, tangos, fox trots, and hesitation waltzes signalled its emergence, and by the time our boys got back from over there America was ready for the jukebox.

No one really knows where the word "jukebox" came from. Until some time in the 30s the jukebox was generally known as the "automatic phonograph." In their authoritative book, *From Tin Foil to Stereo* Oliver Read and Walter Welch claim, "The term had its immediate origin in an old southern word of African origins used among the Negros [*sic*], 'jook,' meaning to dance." Eddie Adlum, publisher of *Replay* magazine suggests it may be a corruption of "jute," and that people who worked the southern jute fields frequented the low-down roadhouses where the automatic phonograph first hit back in the 20s. Thus, jute joint became juke joint, and the music machine became the jute, or juke, box. Adlum also allows what other, less quotable sources opine: That the term had a more overt sexual connotation, like "boogie," and that a juke joint was a whorehouse, a jukebox kept the patrons dancing.

The jukebox owed some of its popularity to neighborhood gathering spots, where it became a permanent feature; and Prohibition may have done more to secure its success there than any other social phenomenon, since every speakeasy had to have music, but not every speak could afford a band.

During Prohibition it was not usual for the house to share in the coin phonograph's take. As far as the distributors were concerned, a proprietor was privileged to have a box in his bar at all, because it helped attract customers and it didn't cost him anything. Although today a "location" might receive as much as 50% of the take, the entertainment value of a well-stocked box itself was the early operator's contribution to a successful social atmosphere.

The automatic phonograph business was affected by the Depression, as nearly every every business was, but a tune on the jukebox still cost only a nickel. Often the music's expense was worth the few minutes's escape. Certainly some jukebox tunes shared among several friends with a nickel apiece to spare was more affordable entertainment than multiple home phonographs with piles of records ever in need of modernizing and replenishing; and relative to other industries, the jukebox flourished in the bad times. With repeal and an official end to the Depression, the jukebox's draw became even greater than it had been. For every speak that closed its illicit doors, a half-dozen bars and restaurants embraced a public eager to demonstrate that happy days really were here again. Every gathering spot had to have its own box, and the quality of that box, and the quality of the music on it, became significant considerations in the minds of patrons and—therefore—establishment owners alike.

Coincidentally, the jukebox became an important influence on the careers of recording artists. In Sousa's day a recording could get by on little more than its presence: The novelty was worth five cents to almost anyone. But by the 30s recorded sound quality had improved, and the jukebox audience listened with an increasingly critical ear.

Moreover, in the 30s and 40s the jukebox provided a musician with the largest audience and the widest exposure he could hope for. For the middle-of-the-road white musician, the direct power of the jukebox in its heyday reflected the importance of record sales made in lots of several hundred at a time to operators with numerous locations. A few such sales could easily inspire a genuine marketing effort on the part of an otherwise taciturn recording company. But for the cowboy and the hillbilly, and especially for the black musician, the jukebox was more than a desirable option. It was often the only way to go. For all practical purposes, there was no place a black musician could have his records heard on a large scale but the jukebox.

In its early years radio was a biased medium, striving for the trappings of respectability. Much early radio music consisted of live concerts staged at fashionable stores by tuxedoed orchestras playing light classics and show tunes. Rhythm and blues, the pop music of the day, was not to be heard over the air. Even when a rare station fiddled around with its format, the R & B it did play was likely to be a form of swing—Roy Milton, Louis Jordan, Buddy Johnson—and not the mean, ribald funk of the era, such as Arthur "Big Boy" Crudup, Tampa Red, Muddy Waters, Bessie Smith, or Roosevelt Sykes.

Since in many places the black population couldn't afford radios in the first place, air play for their music was an academic consideration. But for anyone who wanted to hear "race music" beyond the pale of Harlem's Cotton Club (for white patronage, but for black musicians) or the "Chittlin Circuit" (for black patrons and black musicians), the jukebox was all there was. As a consequence, its presence was essential to any hep establishment's success.

Except for a few anomalous phonographs the jukebox was limited to twenty-four selections until 1948; many models had fewer. And despite a premature assessment by

Homer Capehart when he was general sales manager for Wurlitzer, that twenty-four selections was "all the music we'll ever need on a jukebox," actually, the number is hardly sufficient to exhaust any popular form of music, and certainly not enough to mix-and-match for a variegated clientele. Since people who liked R & B tended to congregate in one spot, people who liked country & western in another, and people who liked swing in yet another, a jukebox operator had to know his customers and place the right kinds of records in the proper locations. A mistake could cost heavily in the box's take, and also make his locations susceptible to "romancing"—attempts by other operators to take over his spots with their boxes. An operator bent on romancing might not rely on another operator's errors, or even on his own claims of better service, more frequent stocking, or some sort of kickback deal. He might also sell the quality of the box.

Since a dependable box was becoming an important feature in any popular gathering place, a box that provided superior service for a greater length of time might be expected to bring in more customers. Unless the owner of a location knew the mechanisms in the various machines, or personally knew the operators in his area, he was unlikely really to know whose box would give him greatest value. One feature he could judge for himself, though, was a jukebox's general appearance. An ugly box had to have some conspicuous redeeming features to remain in one location very long. On the other hand, a pretty box might open up a location that had never accepted recorded music before.

A jukebox ordinarily passed through a three-tiered lifespan. When new it would go to a fancy hotel or restaurant; when replaced by a newer model, it moved on to some respectable family or neighborhood meeting place; finally, bumped again, it went to someplace out of the way, such as a lower class bar or grille. But this schedule did not always prevail. Some locations liked their boxes and held onto them, despite the allure and novelty of something new.

Immediately after the Depression, jukebox sales rose spectacularly. But the machines were built too well to fall apart and did not encourage annual replacement; sales soon leveled off. Wurlitzer dealt with its turnover problems by establishing a unique trade-in policy, offering a \$25-\$50 credit toward one of its own new models to any operator who turned in any make or model jukebox. The factory then destroyed the old box.

Until the middle 30s jukebox cabinets, styled along variously classical lines, were largely made of wood. Then, abruptly, the dimensions of jukebox design underwent a radical change that was as fundamental to the success of the machine in the ensuing decade as anything in the mechanism, the speakers, or the marketing; as important, even as anything on the turntable. In part the change depended on the developing plastics technology that made the new design applications possible. In part it resulted from the rampaging success of the industry in general, which was beginning to demand that some modern sensibility affect the appearance of the machines. And in particular it was due to the peculiar genius of two industrial designers employed by the most prominent jukebox manufacturers of the age.

In 1935, Justus P. Seeburg, the Swedish immigrant who had founded the J. P. Seeburg Piano Company in 1907, hired his son, Noel Marshall Seeburg, to direct his company. Young Seeburg brought several important people into the business with him, one of whom was the deisgner, Nils Miller. Miller immediately began to work with phenolic resins—basically, transformed cellophane—and soon introduced them into Seeburg's jukebox deisgns. At the same time, Paul M. Fuller was experimenting with the same medium over at Wurlitzer. Fuller soon became the leading figure in the history of jukebox design. In the next eleven years, including the four war years when no new jukebox models were manufactured because the factories were all making war-related goods, he designed thirteen full-sized boxes, five table models, one free-standing over-sized table model, and a clutch of speakers. When America's developing war posture precluded the use of metal or plastic decoration, he revitalized the use of wood and glass for jukebox ornamentation. In 1941, for the Wurlitzer Model 850, he employed multiple revolving disks of Polaroid film and variable thicknesses of colorless cellophane to create moving prismatics that changed hues before the onlooker's enchanted eye.

Fuller's artistic temperament seemed ideally suited to the time and the medium in which he worked. Adapting the extreme lines of 1930s art deco influences to the formerly sedate automatic phonograph, he applied light and color and form with a deft hand to a technology that had only recently become adequately sophisticated to make his applications practical. As a material presented itself he used it. In many regards he established the art of jukebox design. His shimmering, sensuous forms made Wurlitzer's jukeboxes instantly recognizable, and in large measure enabled the company to dominate the market until 1948, when Seeburg's engineers produced the first one hundred-selection jukebox.

The jukebox manufacturers were under government constraint to produce war material from May, 1942 until early 1946. The first post-war models to appear from Wurlitzer and Seeburg look like the natural, immediate followups to the pre-war boxes. The very small design changes from their 1941 models to their 1946 models suggest their first post-war boxes were models-in-waiting. They do not begin to reflect the research and development that must have been going on quietly in order to produce the Seeburg M100A and other radical innovations in jukebox design and technology that were just around the corner.

The phenomenal growth and impact of the jukebox industry during the 30s and 40s was not the result of blind chance. There was a need for creative management during this time, and it is no small wonder that Wurlitzer led the industry in those days. Rudolph Wurlitzer emigrated from Germany to Cincinnati, Ohio in 1853, went to work in a music shop, and eventually opened his own business manufacturing musical instruments. In 1880 Rudolph brought his brother Anton to America to assist him, and established a company called Rudolph Wurlitzer & Bro. [*sic*] Anton soon died, but Rudolph moved on into the manufacture of coin-operated machines in 1893.

Rudolph had three sons—Rudolph II, Howard, and Farny R. Farny worked for what was now known as The Rudolph Wurlitzer Company in Cincinnati. He married his secretary, and was forthwith banished to the far reaches of North Tonawanda, New York. There, he was to take over the old DeKleist Barrel Organ Co., and manufacture oompah organs for merry-go-rounds. Farny was extraordinarily successful. The Wurlitzer name, already pre-eminent in the manufacture of player pianos, became nearly as important to carousel music as it would later become to jukebox music.

In 1910 Wurlitzer acquired the Hope-Jones Organ Co., of Elmira, New York, and with it a British genius named Robert Hope-Jones. Hope-Jones had devised a method for removing the organ console from the organ pipes, locating the two parts separately, and activating the pipes electrically from the organ keys. As a result, the organ mechanisms could be hidden from view, while the gorgeous organ console remained fully visible. Soon, Wurlitzer was best known for the massive pipe organs that were used in movie palaces to accompany the silent films of the time, as well as in such reputable establishments as the Eastman School of Music, the Mormon Tabernacle, and Radio City Music Hall, which housed four of the magnificent organs. The Mightly Wurlitzer, as it really was known, helped raise corporate assets to about $6 million by the end of the first world war, placing Wurlitzer in a prime position to bid for the industry's leadership. But when the Depression arrived Wurlitzer was greatly overextended in stock and real estate, and fell into a debt from which it did not recover until 1936. Chief among the reasons for Wurlitzer's recovery and subsequent domination of the jukebox field was Homer E. Capehart.

Capehart's name is associated with four jukebox manufacturers in the years leading up to and encompassing the golden age. In 1921, at the age of 24, he went to work for the Holcomb & Hoke Manufacturing Company; four years later he was sales manager. Holcomb & Hoke made a variety of coin-operated machines. In 1926 the company entered the automatic music machine field with the Electromuse, a sophisticated, continuous-program unit housed in a squared wooden cabinet with a glass front. While the Electromuse sold well, Capehart was ever on the lookout for ways to improve his product. In 1927 he found one—a better record changer, called the Simplex—and bought it on his own. When he showed the mechanism to Holcomb, the boss was annoyed; he had Capehart fired the following day.

Capehart turned around and formed the Capehart Automatic Phonograph Corporation. In October, 1928, he demonstrated the fifty-six selection Capehart Orchestrope at the Chicago Radio Show. The only product that received greater acclaim and attention at that show was television, having its first public outing.

Through the early Depression years Capehart continued to produce high quality automatic coin-operated music machines. But he gambled that the coming phase for phonographs would be in the private home, rather than in the public place, and he lost. Fired from the presidency of his own company, Capehart scraped together what he needed to form the Packard Manufacturing Company in 1932. He did very little with Packard for nearly fifteen years. Instead, in 1933, he approached Farny Wurlitzer with his Simplex record-changing mechanism. The pipe organ business had fallen off as the Depression wore on, and the North Tonawanda factory had been reduced to manufacturing furniture in order to remain in business. Farney was open to a discussion. Capehart had Simplex produce twenty record-changing mechanisms, and Farny had Wurlitzer build twenty console cabinets to accomodate them. When Capehart demonstrated the new instrument to a group of jukebox operators enough of them were swayed by the quality of the new product, and by Capehart's salesmanship, that a new alliance was forged. Capehart became a vice-president and general sales manager for Wurlitzer at a fat salary plus stock options. At last, Homer E. Capehart had the machinery, the company, and the funds to fulfill his destiny.

When Capehart went to work for Wurlitzer there were about 25,000 jukeboxes in operation around the country, and in 1933 Wurlitzer produced only 266 of these. The following year Capehart saw to the production of sixty boxes per week for Wurlitzer alone. In 1935 he increased production to 300 boxes per week, and in 1936, 900 per week. That year, shipping 44,397 jukes, Wurlitzer ran in the black for the first time since the Depression. The all-time one-year company high—45,000 sales—was achieved in 1938.

By the time Capehart resigned from Wurlitzer in 1940 he had established the most formidable distribution network in the history of coin-operated machines. It was so good, in fact, that Capehart himself was unable to crack it when Packard went into serious production in 1946. Although he was a past-master at the game, and although both the Packard

Manhattan and the Packard Pla-Mor were attractively-styled, well-engineered boxes, Capehart barely broke even in this jukebox enterprise. Fortunately, he was already serving his first of three six-year terms as a United States Senator (R.—Indiana) by that time. When Capehart finally lost his senate seat to Birch Bayh in 1962 he bought a 100-selection wall jukebox and once more prepared to enter the business he had known and loved so long. But this time Farny Wurlitzer bought out Packard, and ended Homer E. Capehart's forty-year-long association with the world of the jukebox.

Capehart's—and, therefore, Wurlitzer's—principal competition during the golden age was provided by the J. P. Seeburg Piano Company, and by the Rockola Manufacturing Corporation. Seeburg had Nils Miller and M. W. Kenney, the brilliant engineer largely responsible for Seeburg's revolutionary breakthrough into the hundred-selection M100A in 1948. Still, while Seeburg was a manufacturer of enormous ability, he could not yet crack Capehart's lock on the industry.

Neither could David C. Rockola, the Canadian-born manufacturer. Rockola made his early success in weighing machines. In 1930, seeing a future in coin-operated mechanisms, he invested heavily in a pinball game called "Juggleball," and lost his shirt. Called on the carpet by his creditors, he challenged them with the classic businessman's reply: They could close him down and take nickels on their dollars, or back him up and get everything that was owed. They backed him. Four years later Rockola was out of debt. He picked up the patents held by the old John Gabel Company, designed his own new cabinets, and joined the jukebox industry in a big way. Rock-ola contended with Seeburg for the number two spot after Wurlitzer in the late 30s and early 40s, and then contended with Wurlitzer for the number two spot after Seeburg in the 50s. Today, Wurlitzer no longer produces jukeboxes; Seeburg, trust-busted under the Sherman Act in the middle 50s, is bankrupt; AMI has merged with Rowe. Of all the major jukebox manufacturers from the golden age, only Rock-ola still produces jukeboxes.

Since the introduction of Seeburg's M100A in 1948, the jukebox industry has undergone profound changes in design, manufacturing techniques, and distribution practices. It has seen, and in large measure determined the outcome of, wars among the record companies that resulted in the replacement of 78 rpm disks by 33s and 45s; 200-selection boxes; video jukes; computer games; the rise of foreign manufacturers. But the jukebox's modern history, like that of its more classic era, has been only partly documented; and by now the complete story is lost in dissolutions, mergers, bankruptcies, law suits, and deaths. The last great hope for sorting out the whole linear tale went up in smoke in 1974, when Wurlitzer closed its doors on the phenomenon it had helped create, and fed its body of records to the fire. Boxes of promotional literature went, and machine parts, and original brochures, and files: All gone. And the people with solid recollections of Seeburg, Mills, Packard—even the small houses like Filben, Jennings, or Buckley: Gone. And the men who made the jukebox industry—entrepreneurs, industrialists, designers, salesmen—gone, mostly without telling their stories. We are left with indifferent records, and specimens of the hard evidence: The jukeboxes themselves.

It's for the jukeboxes that the spate of new collectors have appeared, and a good thing they have. These are the people who, seeking out spare bubble tubes for one machine, or needle changers for another, will come across the charm, in artifact and tale, that makes the machines more than simply pretty record-changing devices.

There's no formal training for jukebox collectors; they're just people whose interest expands into a hobby, then expands some more until they find themselves part of an intricately connected web of people who share their original interest. "Before you know it you've got too many jukeboxes and not enough cash," notes Steve Loots, publisher of a jukebox collector's newsletter, *Victory Glass.* Enough cash, of course, is an essential component of the collecting hobby. More essential every day.

Nineteen-forty-six—the first year of postwar jukebox production—was also the biggest year in the industry to that time. Seeburg brought out the first new jukebox anyone had seen in four years—the S 146, known fondly as the "trash can" or "barrel"—and, given his head after four years of wartime shutdown, Wurlitzer's Paul Fuller produced the single best-known, best-loved jukebox of all time, the Model 1015. The 1015 had the pizzazz people were looking for, and Wurlitzer shipped more than 56,000 during late 1946 and 1947, accompanied by the largest promotional campaign in jukebox history. In an age when the name of a box could determine the success or failure of a bar or restaurant, napkins, swizzle sticks, coasters, decals, tabletops, national magazine advertisements, and billboards across the land proclaimed, and persuaded America, that "Wurlitzer is Juke Box."

When first manufactured, the 1015 was sold to distributors for about $750, less quantity discounts which could range as high as 40%. In the following 20 years prices fluctuated downward, and 1015s could be bought for as little as $35 in the early 60s. The same jukebox cost close to $300 ten years later, and as of 1980 a Model 1015 in restored condition brought as much as $6500. To a greater or lesser extent, the same kinds of price increases hold true for every jukebox pictured in this book. In professional antique dealers' terms they are now "collectible": Old enough and rare enough and of sufficient quality to have intrinsic worth that will lead them to be valuable as antiques when they reach 100 years.

Many people involved in buying, restoring, selling, and trading classic jukeboxes are in it for the money. It isn't only that, nor is it just that people seem to want what other people want. Jukeboxes also have sentimental value. All kinds of people have memories of jukeboxes, and buy the restored classics of their own jukebox days: Movie producers, rock 'n' roll stars, doctors, lawyers, old-time hips, assembly-line workers—they will not fit into a single category. Usually one box or two will satisfy the dream. But sometimes a first one sparks a dangerous fire that develops into an acquisitive habit, and the second box leads to a third, the third to weekends spent scouring byways and back alleys looking for more, picking up some information, talking—"juking."

One collector whose house holds about 65 of the best classic boxes, has touched the thread that seems to connect everyone involved with the contemporary appreciation of classic light-up jukeboxes: "It must be some kind of tie to my past that I can dream about but never quite put my finger on. On a good day I can get back to those years. It seems it was an easier time for me. The world was half playing, I knew I was going to get a warm meal in my belly, and these jukeboxes were around. I saw them. I remember. They left an indelible mark. And the memories mean so much to me that my involvement with them is permanent."

In a sense, that is what this book is about: Not all the jukebox years, stretching back to Edison more than a century ago; but merely the best of them. Only the years when the design was richest, the sales figures highest, the influence most pronounced, and the voice of the jukebox was heard throughout the land.

Full-Sized Jukeboxes

If tonight you are dancing with your darling in the ruby-laser glow of digits on a computer jukebox screen, you may remember this as one of the golden years of the jukebox. And if you were a jukebox operator in the early 1950s, when hundred-selection boxes competed with two-hundred-selection boxes and overran the sweet shoppes and the bars, you may remember those as golden years.

For most jukebox collectors and devotees, however, the golden age began in 1937 with the introduction of illuminated plastics; and it ended abruptly in 1949 when Paul Fuller suffered his first serious heart attack and Seeburg introduced its bulky but highly serviceable M100A, the first hundred-selection juke.

The thirty-two full-sized jukeboxes whose photographs follow are the golden cream of the golden age. They appear here chronologically, from 1937 through 1948.

20

WURLITZER Model 24

This 1937 model was one of the first Wurlitzer jukeboxes to offer 24 selections instead of 12 or 16, and it prompted the ordinarily perceptive Homer E. Capehart to opine, "That's all the music we'll ever need on a jukebox." He was very wrong, of course; but he was very right for the ensuing decade. The Model 24 was also the first jukebox to incorporate illuminated plastics into its design. The company's transition from the heavy wooden radio cabinets it had used in the past to a bright and modern deco line helped to establish Wurlitzer's pre-eminence in the coin-operated phonograph industry.

WURLITZER
WURLITZER
MULTI-SELECTOR

22
WURLITZER Model 500

The first machine in the industry to use rotating color cylinders, the Model 500 was also one of the first, along with the Model 600, to introduce the keyboard selector. According to the company's 1938-39 brochure, "Hardest nut for the music merchant to crack has proved to be the white collar and tails type of location frankly and swankly catering to the carriage trade. Few phonographs found welcome in this ultra ultra atmosphere until the advent of the Wurlitzer Deluxe 500."

WURLITZER

24

WURLITZER Model 600

Slightly smaller and less elaborate than the Model 500, this second of Wurlitzer's 1938-39 jukeboxes could be equipped with either a keyboard or a rotary selector. The keyboard version had a unique green arrow that could spin and indicate to the patron which of its 24 selections was playing. In the rotary model selector buttons were located in the green arrow's place. By 1939 Wurlitzer had shipped 9,777 of the Model 600, and boasted in its brochure, "Combining the brilliant eye-catching beauty of fine woods, gleaming metals, and colorful illuminated plastics with masterful living tone, the Wurlitzer 600 has scored the most sensational success in the history of automatic music. It's by far America's most popular phonograph."

WURLITZER
RECORD NOW PLAYING

26
AMI Streamliner

Manufactured in 1938-39, the Streamliner was one of the very first light-up jukeboxes. Its Lumiline incandescent light tube, set behind the vertical center bar in front of the speaker, was a forerunner of the modern fluorescent light.

28

AMI Singing Tower

With 20 selections on 10 disks, the 1939 Singing Towers was the first jukebox whose mechanism was capable of playing both sides of a single record. It was also the first jukebox whose speaker was mounted horizontally. Sound, reflected up off the dome, showered the patrons, creating the effect of music coming from all sides. Excepting the program selector bars, which were plastic, everything transparent on this box was ¾" glass, including the top dome. Due to the peculiarities of reflection, the mirrors that run down the center of the box appear black in this photograph.

Singing Towers

30
MILLS Empress

Mills Industries, formerly the Mills Novelty Co., was one of the oldest jukebox manufacturers in the world when economic difficulties forced it into chapter eleven bankruptcy in 1948. Little reliable information has been available concerning the organization since that time. This stolid, 1939 jukebox gained some popularity despite the fact that its record changing mechanism could not be seen. The die-cast, deco, pot metal facing accompanied several different color combinations of the marbelized plastic that made up the body of the box.

1 2 3 4 5 6 7 8 9 10 11 12 13 14 15 16 17 18 19 20

32
MILLS Throne of Music

Released the same year as the Mills Empress, 1939, the Throne of Music also achieved a modest popularity despite the fact that its record changing mechanism could not be seen.

Record Now Playing
1 2 3 4 5 6 7 8 9 10 11 12 13 14 15 16 17 18 19 20
MILLS

34
ROCK-OLA Master Rockolite

Until World War II, the record-changing mechanisms could not be seen on Rock-Ola jukeboxes. This 1940 model, sometimes called the Luxury Light-up, was one of the company's best-known boxes in the pre-war era.

Rock-Ola

36

WURLITZER Model 700

In the pre-war years of 1940 and 1941, Paul Fuller designed five separate and distinct full-sized jukeboxes in a series that included the Models 700, 750, 780, 800, and 850. Wurlitzer sold 9,498 of this, the economy model in the 1940 line. The company's glowing promotional copy read, "On the model 700, pilasters of rich Italian onyx may be illuminated either by using bulbs of varying colors to attain a rich blending of shades, or by bulbs of a single color to match the predominate note of the location's decorator scheme. On either side of the cabinet, sweeping back to the top of the pilaster, plastic panels glow with an exquisite green—put the finishing touches to another Wurlitzer triumph in glamour lighting."

SPECIAL
6 PLAYS FOR 25¢
QUARTERS ONLY
WURLITZER
25¢ 10¢ 5¢

38
WURLITZER Model 800

The last of Wurlitzer's exclusively mechanical selection jukes, 1940's deluxe Model 800 featured three bubble tubes in its center pilasters and the longest color cylinders Wurlitzer ever used, surrounding incandescent bulbs in its side pilasters. Light from a rotating color cylinder was broken up by zebra-striped acetate on the back of the pilaster, making it flicker like live fire.

WURLITZER

40

WURLITZER Model 750

With 18,387 units shipped, the Model 750 was the most popular of Wurlitzer's 1941 jukeboxes. It featured two small, curved bubble tubes beneath the selector buttons, and a choice of either a mural or an illuminated plastic backdrop on the back door behind the record changing mechanism. Although early boxes in the run had only mechanical selectors, which accepted coins after a patron had chosen the music, Wurlitzer added an electric selection option later in the year on the Model 750 E, which accepted coins before selections were made. The Model 750 was about 5" shorter and 5" narrower than the other pre-war Wurlitzer models, and its small, convenient size may have contributed to its success.

WURLITZER
25¢
10¢
5¢

42

WURLITZER Model 780

For obvious reasons, the Model 780 was known as the Wagon Wheel. Wurlitzer's 1941 brochure explains that it is "styled to harmonize with the finest furnishings. Early American from its Governor Winthrop cabinet to its pewter finished hardware; from its spinning wheel grille with colorful patch-work background to its butterfly peg construction, the rich conservative beauty of this instrument marks a decided departure from the 'commercial' appearance of all other automatic phonographs."

WURLITZER
25¢ 10¢ 5¢

44

WURLITZER Model 850

Described by its manufacturer as "the only super deluxe phonograph in the industry," the 1941 Model 850—also known as the Peacock—introduced Polarized film on a commercial scale; it is still the only jukebox ever to have used the film. The machine's Polarizer unit was made of two spinning, Polarized acetate disks with three incandescent light bulbs behind each one. The Polaroid film interacted with the plastic to create a prism effect, breaking up the white light from the bulb and producing colors. As the discs spun, the colors changed. The front door of the machine was a sandwich composed of the front glass with the peacock image screened onto it; the analyzer, which kept the image from showing black spots; the Polaroid film; and a final sheet of clear glass. As Wurlitzer claimed at the time of its release, there was "nothing like it ever on any phonograph."

WURLITZER

46

SEEBURG Classic

True to its name, this early 1940s Seeburg model was a representative jukebox for its time. Except for the clear glass pilasters flanking the green center strip, the entire body was made of wood and molded plastic. And, as with most of the Seeburg models that preceded the M100A in 1948, the Classic's changer mechanism was not visible.

SEEBURG
25¢
10¢
5¢

48

SEEBURG 9800

Like those of Rock-Ola's Spectravox and AMI's Singing Towers, the speakers of the 9800 faced up, projecting their sounds against the outside face of a hidden metal funnel that reflected the music out into the room. This early 1940s box had a single color cylinder located behind the glass door at its front. Its softly-lit vertical bars were known as candlelight pilasters.

Seeburg

50
ROCK-OLA Spectravox

A patron dialed the selection on the 1941-2 Spectravox as he would dial a telephone call, and music came out the top—under, not through, the bowl, which acted as a sound deflector and diffused the music. But tucked away somewhere else, behind the bar or in a closet, the actual record changing and playing mechanism was housed in an unremarkable-looking cabinet called the Playmaster. The surface of the Spectravox was painted to look like wood grain. Corrugated steel running up the center and sides reflected red light-up plastic.

Rock-Ola

52
WURLITZER Model 950

When the United States went to war, the jukebox manufacturers stopped producing coin-operated music machines, and retooled for wartime production. As a result, only about 3400 of the Model 950 were shipped in 1942, making this one of the most difficult jukeboxes of the era to locate today. The Model 950 was the first Wurlitzer jukebox to use fluorescent tubes, and the first to use long bubble tubes, in the side pilasters. Internal mirrors, angled at 45°, made the gazelles on the box's face change colors as the pilasters did. Because metal was in short supply as production on this box began, many of its internal components, including the coin chutes, coin box, and tone arm post, were made of wood.

INSERT ONE OR MORE COINS
WURLITZER
THEN MAKE SELECTIONS

54

SEEBURG Envoy

One of a sequence of relatively similar boxes manufactured by Seeburg in the 1940s, including the Crown, Cadet, Major, Vogue, Casino, and Mayfair, the Envoy had an air-brushed base and marbleized plastic at its top. Glass pilasters stood beside a wider pilaster above the speaker.

RECORD
PLAYING
SEEBURG

56
WURLITZER Model 42

During the war, all the principal coin machine manufacturers released "Victory" models of one sort or another. The Model 42 was Wurlitzer's contribution from 1942-1945. Instead of a complete jukebox the company shipped only a new cabinet, which could be adapted for use with any of several selector mechanisms from the early 1930s pre-light-up boxes, the 1938-39 Model 500, or the 1938-39 Model 600. The war also had an impact on the cabinet's cosmetics: There was no plastic used anywhere on the Model 42. The mirrors and everything transparent were glass.

WURLITZER

58

ROCK-OLA Commando

Because plastic was scarce during the war, all the transparent parts of this rare 1942 jukebox were glass, except the three red panels in the bottom section. The lower casing was bird's-eye maple. The Commando was an unusual Rock-Ola model also in that its record changing mechanism, like that of the Master Rockolite, was not visible to the patron. Four separate doors in the front of the box opened to allow the operator to repair the machine or to change its records.

ROCK-OLA

60
WURLITZER Model 1015

Complete with color wheels in its sides, new die castings, formed plastics, and the bubble tubes it helped make famous running from its base to its arch, the Model 1015 was the single most popular jukebox of the light-up era. Wurlitzer shipped more than 56,000 1015s in 1946 and 1947, accompanied by the largest promotional campaign in jukebox history, including swizzle sticks, napkins, tabletops, coasters, decals, billboards, and prominent advertisements in national magazines, all proclaiming "Wurlitzer is Juke Box."

WURLITZER

62

ROCK-OLA Model 1422

The first in the "MAGIC GLO" series of three boxes Rock-Ola manufactured immediately after the war, the 1946 model had two color cylinders lit by incandescent bulbs behind its wooden grille, and two more in its side pilasters lit by fluorescent tubes. The top plastic was illuminated by another fluorescent tube, and the shoulders were lit by more incandescent bulbs. A stylized 18th century European courting scene was screened onto the plastic backdrop surrounding the chrome-plated record stack on three sides. After the patron made his selection the stack kicked out the appropriate record tray, and the turntable rose to receive the disk.

64

AMI Model A

Also known as the Mother of Plastic, this 1946 model was the first jukebox to make extensive use of acrylic plastics, and the first to use colored fluorescent lights. In fact, the only incandescent light used in this box was a single, long bulb in the column below the coin return slot, that illuminated the red, green, and blue glass jewels. Two color cylinders, one on either side of the base of the box, were activated when the motor started, so that a patron's coin bought sights as well as sounds. But the turntable would not begin to revolve until all the machine's tubes had warmed up. As a result, each record started at its true volume, instead of starting softly and growing louder through the first few bars of music.

66
PACKARD Manhattan

The 1946 Packard Manhattan was the deluxe model of the two full-sized, high-quality jukeboxes produced by Homer E. Capehart while he served as a United States Senator (R.—Indiana). The cabinet was made of burled wood, the window was etched glass, the mechanism was completely chromed; black musical notes were screened onto yellow glass inside the cabinet. The Manhattan played one side of each of 24 disks, selected on a protruding wheel that was and is unique to Packard boxes.

"MANHATTAN"

68

ROCK-OLA Model 1426

A paint called frost was used to screen the musical notes motif onto the front window; on some unrestored boxes it is still possible to rub the paint off with a finger. The center strip in front of the speaker was metal instead of wood; the grille lit up in four colors instead of five; only two color cylinders were used in the side pilasters, there were none behind the grille; and the mural behind the record changing mechanism was a quilted gold cloth with jeweled mirrors. In all other respects this, Rock-Ola's 1947 jukebox, was identical to the 1946 Model 1422.

ROCK-OLA

70
PACKARD Pla-Mor

This jukebox was Packard's economy model for 1946. Small, incandescent bulbs illuminated radically deep molded plastics. A musical motif, screened onto sheet plastic, backed a complex changer mechanism that kicked the selection from a horizontal stack and passed it to a second record holder, which placed the disk on the turntable. Like the Manhattan, Packard's Pla-Mor played one side each of 24 records, selected on the unique Packard wheel.

PACKARD
PLA MOR

72

AMI Model B

A toned-down version of the Mother of Plastic, this 1947 jukebox played 40 selections on 20 disks. It used two color wheels in the lower pilasters, and a third in the upper pilaster. It was one of the last jukeboxes available exclusively for 78 rpm records.

74
WURLITZER Ambassador

The Ambassador, introduced in 1947 and used in general circulation for about five years, was one of many kits manufacturers provided that allowed operators to supply new boxes for their locations without having to purchase completely new machines. Kits were especially popular during the war, when jukebox shortages doubled and trebled the prices of whole units. Like the other kits, the Ambassador was strictly a cosmetic change. It was designed to accommodate the workings of the Model 1015, and was distinguised from its famous counterpart chiefly in its lack of bubble tubes. The Ambassador was among the first jukeboxes engineered by operators to demand ten cents per play.

WURLITZER

76

WURLITZER Model 1080

Although this 1947-1948 model contained all the mechanical refinements of the earlier Model 1015, its less dazzling appearance made it an appropriate choice for relatively conservative locations. Wurlitzer sold 7,604 of this box, known as the Colonial, advising that "Its graceful colonial styled cabinet is a period master piece rich in old world charm. Its illuminated mirror plastics have the glow and sparkle of fine cut glass. An early American lyre inspired its colorful grille. Its visible record changer reproduces a famous 18th century painting." Wurlitzer also produced a Model 1080-A, which was identical to the 1080 cosmetically, but contained the Model 1100 sound system.

WURLITZER

78
SEEBURG S-148

Following the S-146 (1946) and the S-147 (1947), this 1948 jukebox was the third and rarest in a series of three with identical body shapes known as the Trashcan or the Barrel. It was distinguished from its predecessors by its blond, wood-grained metal cabinet (the S-146 was made of brown wood; the S-147 was made of dark wood-grained metal) and its fluted white dome (the S-146 had a smooth pink dome; the S-147 had a smooth white dome). In addition, the S-148 was the only box of the three to use a color cylinder in its dome and at the bottom of its grille as well.

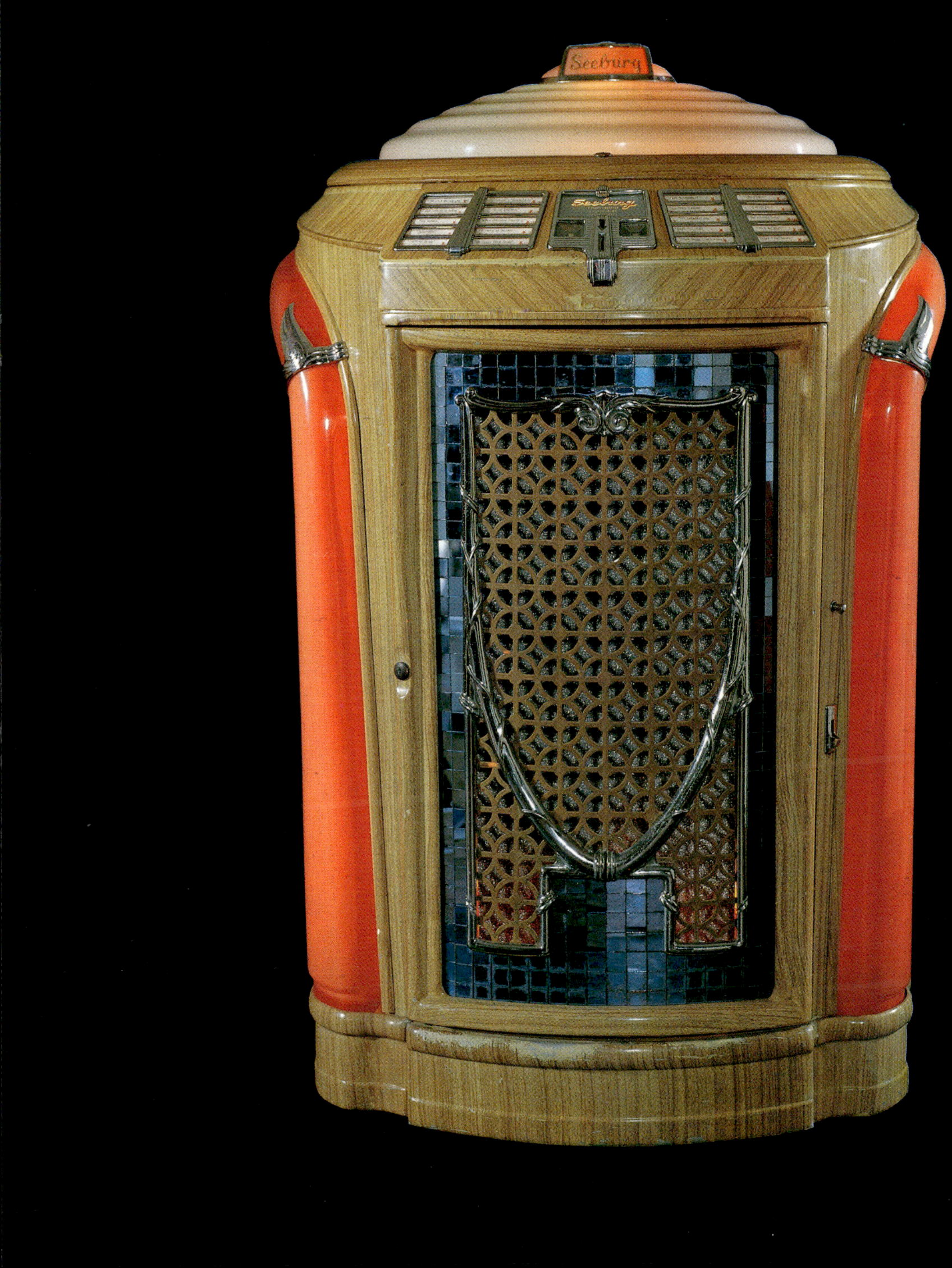
Seeburg

80
ROCK-OLA Model 1428

The deep ruby plastic was rippled and rolled on its sides; the pale green was textured. The body of the box was wood, but its front door was blond-grained metal. A single color cylinder stood in the center of the box. Internally, Rock-Ola's 1948 jukebox was essentially the same as its Models 1422 and 1426 of the two previous years.

82

WURLITZER Model 1100

Because of the phenomenal success of its Model 1015, Wurlitzer miscalculated the demand for this last jukebox ever designed by Paul Fuller: Only 7,000 were shipped, many were returned, and others never left the assembly line. This 1948-49 model was the first jukebox to use a lightweight plastic tone arm, and the first to use a ceramic cartridge rather than a magnetic one—requiring the first use of a pre-amp in jukebox history. As a result of its mechanical innovations, the Model 1100 reduced record wear while improving fidelity. The selector bar rotated when pressed, offering the patron a view of eight selections at a time, numbered 1-8, 9-16, and 17-24. Audience participation may have been part of Wurlitzer's plan. Its brochure announced, "The 1100 is more fun to watch! Because its great plastic panoramic sky-top turret window will draw people like a magnet. Your customers will watch the mechanism work. Now, as never before, this wide open bomber-nose window gives them an unobstructed view. It puts them right where you want them—next to the coin slide."

1 2 3 4
5 6 7 8
24
WURLITZER

Jukebox Table Models

Wurlitzer manufactured complete boxes small enough to fit on stands or tables, and Rock-Ola produced two table model boxes complete except for speakers. Nearly all these table models were released when records cost only a nickel to play; consequently, almost all of them accept no coin but the five-cent piece.

Most table model jukes were 12-selection boxes and they used one of two record-changing mechanisms. The one used by Wurlitzer was mechanical rather than electric. It stacked a dozen records from which the patron made his choice before inserting any money. When the coin rolled down the chute the entire stack of disks moved up or down until the selection reached the level of the tone arm. Then rods or posts with washers lifted the entire pile of records above the selection, leaving room for the tone arm to slide over and play the chosen tune.

Rock-Ola's table models used the same mechanical principles that were featured in the company's full-sized boxes: The chosen record, still in its tray, slid out and away from the stack. The turntable rose up beneath it and carried the record up to the tone arm, returning it to its tray, and the tray to the stack, after the tone arm lifted up again at the end of the record.

TABLE MODELS

WURLITZER Model 50

This was the only completely free-standing table jukebox ever made. Its grille rods were colored with yellow gels that allowed light to shoot through the plastic on the three exposed sides. Its back door mural was three-dimensional, made of painted wooden half-rounds. (Left)

ROCK-OLA Model 39-A

Rock-Ola devoted its efforts to full-sized jukeboxes. This 1939 model was one of only two table units the company ever made. (Right)

WURLITZER

TABLE MODELS

WURLITZER Model 41

The pilasters visible in this front-on photograph were repeated at the rear of the unit. This 1940-41 box opened for servicing at the center metal bar. (Left top)

WURLITZER Model 51

The rarest of all Wurlitzer table models, the Model 51 was also the only Wurlitzer table model ever made without illuminated plastics. Manufactured in 1937, its wooden case reflected the feeling of early 30s pre-light-up jukebox design. (Right top)

WURLITZER Model 61

The most common of all the classic Wurlitzer table models featured wood-grained metal escutcheons on the upper half of its case. It was produced in 1938-39. (Left bottom)

WURLITZER Model 71

Except that the yellow plastic was marbleized, the horn design in this 1940-41 table juke was replicated in the Model 81—which is generally considered to be the most attractive, most desirable and most collectible. Like its nearly identical counterpart, the Model 71 accepted nickels, dimes, and quarters. (Right bottom)

WURLITZER

Jukebox Speakers

While table model jukeboxes were manufactured and distributed with the same kind of attention to year and model number that accompanied the production of full-sized boxes, speaker unit years are not clearly defined, for the most part. Auxiliary speaker units were less formal pieces of furniture than the boxes; most were equipped neither with selection nor with record-changing capabilities; and they are most conveniently divided simply into pre- and post-war models.

SPEAKERS

Wurlitzer Pre-War Wooden Case

Model 160

Wurlitzer designed this auxiliary speaker to complement the full-sized Model 780, the Wagon Wheel. It was intended to suit a wide variety of locations "becuase of its conservative styling and design." (Top)

Model 210

Similar to the Model 220, except for its flat top, this speaker has a wooden case with wooden bars that reach horizontally across the speaker cloth. At the base the illuminated plastic grille is emblazoned with the Wurlitzer logo. (Left bottom)

Model 220

The plastic "Music" plate was the only illuminated part of this wooden speaker. (Right bottom)

WURLITZER
WURLITZER
WURLITZER
MUSIC

SPEAKERS

Wurlitzer Pre-War Wooden Case

Model 39-A

The case of this speaker was all wood except the word plates at top and bottom which were illuminated plastic. The Model 39 said, "Music by/Wurlitzer," rather than "Strike Up the Band/Wurlitzer." (Right bottom)

Model 250

The red uprights were painted wood, but the word plates were light-up plastic. The speaker was manufactured in two versions. One—the 250—was connected with the jukebox by cable wires; the other—the 350, identical in appearance—employed a so-called "wireless" transformer, which allowed it to run on the standard house current. (Left top)

MUSIC BY
WURLITZER

SPEAKERS

Wurlitzer Pre-War Light-Up

Model 420

With its painted glass pilasters the Model 420 was essentially the Model 430, except that it had no remote selection unit. (Left)

Model 430

Manufactured in 1942, this last in Wurlitzer's pre-war line of speakers was intended to accompany the full-sized Model 950. It was an unusual speaker in that it accepted coins. It had a remote selection unit as well, but contained no record playing or changing mechanism. Very few of these speakers survived through the years with their glass pilasters intact. (Right)

SPEAKERS

Wurlitzer Pre-War Light-Up

Model 580

Perhaps the loveliest of all auxiliary speaker units, the Model 580 was the only speaker ever to have bubble tubes, which made up its flower stems. Intended to accompany Wurlitzer's full-sized Model 850A, the speaker had a full selecting unit and coin box, but neither an amplifier nor any record-changing mechanism.

WURLITZER
MUSIC

SPEAKERS

Wurlitzer Post-War

Model 4000

This speaker case was a simple nickel-plated star. It could be hung on the wall or ceiling. (Left top)

Model 4002

Identical to the Model 4000, except for the colored plastic that replaced the pot metal star. Both speakers were available with a chrome star backed by metal, as well as with the flocked Wurlitzer "W" on the grille cloth. (Right top)

Model 4003

The case was wood painted pale blue. The red Wurlitzer scroll projected light upward from a small-watt bulb. The musical note motif was screened onto the case. (Left bottom)

Model 4004

The Johnny One-Note logo was prominently displayed in red plastic on this wood-cased speaker. Black and yellow parts were painted metal. The speaker was not illuminated in any way. (Right bottom)

WURLITZER
WURLITZER
MUSIC

SPEAKERS
Wurlitzer Post-War

Model 4005

An unadorned, unilluminated plain wooden round speaker. (Left top)

Model 4006

A virtually identical mirror-faced version of the Model 4005. (Right top)

Model 4007

This large oval speaker was more than 2½' high. The Johnny One-Note logo was vacuum-formed to protrude three-dimensionally from the speaker. A color wheel behind the logo threw light up behind the plastic Wurlitzer name plate and against the mirrors. (Left bottom)

Model 4008

This most elaborate speaker of the post-war period could be mounted either on the ceiling or on the wall. It was mirrored on the inside and at the center hub, where a color wheel tinted the interior mirrors as the hub itself revolved. The red, yellow, and green plastic parts were illuminated. The use of polished aluminum echoed the design of the full-sized Model 1015, as did the top of this speaker. (Right bottom)

WURLITZER

WURLITZER
Music

WURLITZER

104
SPEAKERS
Rock-Ola

Tonette

An early non-illuminated wall speaker with a bakelite grille. (Right bottom)

Chandelier

The case was intended to hang from the ceiling. The speaker faced down so that sound could radiate into the room. A color cylinder inside the case revolved, changing the colors of the plastic side panels. (Right top)

Organ Type

The case was about 5' high, and designed to hang up off the floor, wedged into a corner of a room so that the walls on both its back sides could reflect sound into the room. The speaker was located in the top of the case. (Left)

Moderne

Similar to the Organ Type, this speaker also was intended to hang in a corner of a room. (Center)

ROCK-OLA

ROCK-OLA
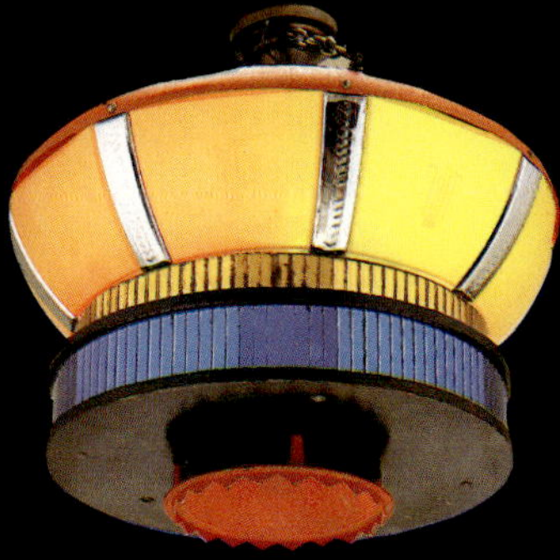

ROCK-OLA

106
SPEAKERS
Seeburg

Except, perhaps, as documented in internal records which have been lost, Seeburg is not known to have named its speakers or to have assigned them externally useful model numbers in most cases. The company made many versions of the Speak-O-Gram, most of which included organ pipes in some configuration. The organ pipes were strictly cosmetic, since the speaker itself was placed behind the center grille in these pre-war units. The metal-cased speaker with blue mirrors was manufactured immediately after the war, and was intended to provide auxiliary sound for the Models 146, 147, and 148—the Trashcan.

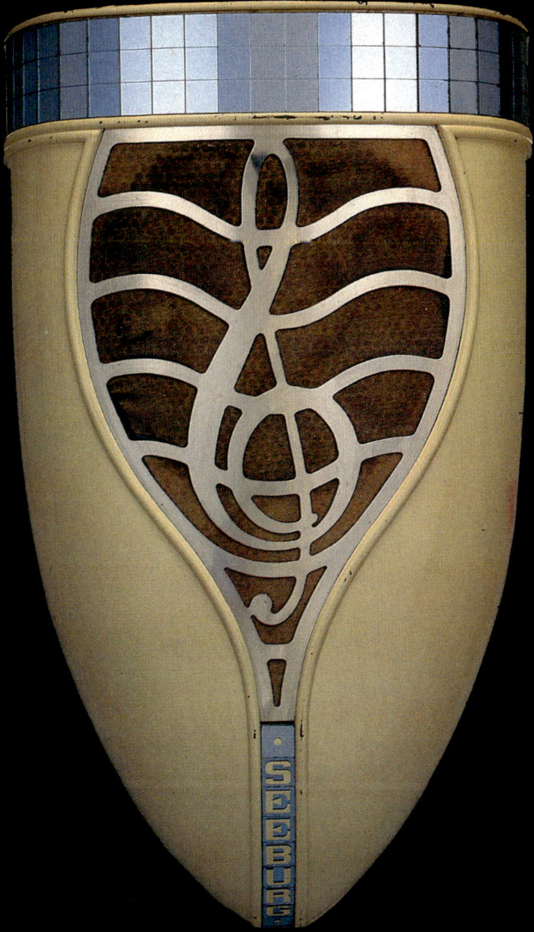
SEEBURG

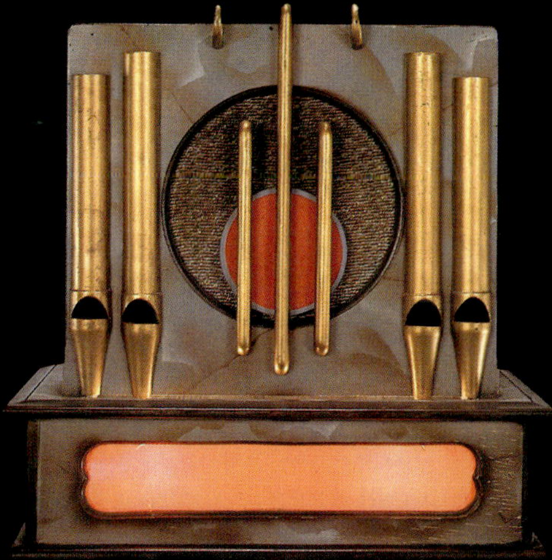

SPEAKERS
Packard

Like Seeburg and AMI, Packard is not known to have numbered or named its speaker units. The company produced numerous speakers to accompany its hide-away boxes, but their design often resembled that of Packard's two full-sized jukes, the Manhattan and the Pla-Mor.

PACKARD
PLA-MOR

Epilogue

Seeburg broke Wurlitzer's lock on the industry when it introduced the first 100-selection jukebox, in 1948. Nils Miller's hard, angular, chromium-trimmed design was as radical a departure from the boxes of the golden age as the first colorful light-up machines had been from the sedate radio cabinets of the 1920s and 30s. Numerous jukebox operators defected from Wurlitzer, placing Seeburg's machine in the best locations, and placing Seeburg at the forefront of the industry.

SEEBURG M-100A

Any copy of this book issued by the publisher as a paperback is sold subject to the condition that it shall not by way of trade or otherwise, be lent, re-sold, hired out or otherwise circulated, without the publisher's prior consent, in any form of binding or cover other than that in which it is published, and without a similar condition including these words being imposed on a subsequent purchaser.

First published in Great Britain in 1981
by Thames and Hudson Ltd, London

Copyright ©1981 Lancaster-Miller, Inc.

All Rights Reserved. No part of this publication may be reproduced or transmitted in any form or by any means, electronic or mechanical, including photocopy, recording or any information storage and retrieval system, without permission in writing from the publisher.

Printed and bound in Japan